MECHANIC MOTOR VEHICLE SECOND YEAR MCQ

OBJECTIVE QUESTION ANSWERS

MANOJ DOLE

Digitization is the need of the time. In the future, training in industrial training institutes will need to be conducted using online internet to make training more convenient and easy. E-books containing a set of MCQ questions will be made available to the trainees as they need to be more accustomed to the multiple choice questions MCQ to prepare for the online exams taking place in their industrial training institutes.

With all these factors in mind, Mr. Manoj Madhukar Dole Instructor, Industrial Training Institute, Satara, has written books according to the new annual system and NSQF-5 syllabus. And they've created theoretical mobile apps and blogs to make training easier, and made all these educational materials available for download on the world famous websites Google Play Store, Amazon and Apple Book Store.

The books were published by Hon'ble Joint Director Shri Rajendra Ghume Saheb Regional Office of Vocational Education and Training, Pune on 9/1/2019, at this time Shri Prakash Saigavkar Saheb Principal Government Industrial Training Institute Aundh Pune, Shri Tukaram Misal Saheb Principal Govt. Q. Sanstha Satara, Shri Sachin Dhumal Saheb District Vocational Education and Training Officer Satara, Shri Yatin Pargaonkar Saheb Principal Govt. Q. Sanstha Kolhapur, Shri Vikas Teke Saheb Inspector Vocational Education and Training Regional Office Pune, Palekar Foods Products Pvt. Ltd. Entrepreneurial Chairman of Satara Mr. Nilkanthrao Palekar Saheb, Chairman of Hira Foods Mr. Ibrahim Baba Tamboli Saheb, Mrs. Shalmali Pawar Headmaster Government Technical School Center Satara and other dignitaries were present on the occasion.

Contents

Prologue

Mechanic Motor Vehicle (MMV) B is a simple Book for ITI Engineering Course Mechanic Motor Vehicle (MMV) , Second Year, Sem- 3 & 4, Revised NSQ F-5 Syllabus in 2022, It contains objective questions with underlined & bold correct answers MCQ covering all topics including all about light vehicle/Heavy Vehicle transmission units including Gear box, Single plate clutch assembly, Diaphragm clutch assembly , Constant mesh Gear box, synchromesh gear box, gear linkages, Propeller shaft, Universal Slip Joint, Rear axle assembly, Differential assembly, light vehicle Chassis units, Shackle, Leaf spring, Front axle, Front and rear suspension, Steering Gearbox- worm and roller type, Steering Gearbox- Reticulating ball type, Master cylinder, Tandem Master cylinder, Front and rear brake, Wheel cylinder , Vacuum booster, Air servo unit, Air tank (reservoir), wheel balancing and Wheel Alignment, Electronic Control Unit, charging system, starting system, Vehicle Air Conditioning system, Traffic Regulations and lots more.

We add new question answers with each new version. Please email us in case of any errors/omissions.

Foreword

Vocational education and training is imparted through the Department of Vocational Education and Training through the Department of Business Education and Business Practical to supply multi-skilled artisans in line with the rapidly growing demand in the industrial sector in the 21st century. All the occupations within the institutions are important, as the trainees from these occupations develop multi-skills as per the demands of the industry.

with the noble intention of making available MCQ e-books suitable for all businesses, considering that all the examinations in all the industries in the industrial sector are conducted online and include MCQ method questions. Mr. Manoj Madhukar Dole has written a very good e-book on MCQ method as per the new annual syllabus. This e-book will definitely be a guide for all the trainees, trainee candidates, training instructors and others concerned.

The author of the book is Mr. Manoj Madhukar Dole, Instructor Gov. ITI Satara has 17 years of training experience. Written as a new annual pattern, this e-book incorporates modern digital QR Code technology to understand the layout, simple language, and simple syntax, diagrams and videos for each subject. So I am sure that this e-book will definitely be useful for in-depth study and exam practice. The work they have done is certainly commendable.

Mr. Tukaram Misal
Principal Government Industrial Training Institute Satara.

Preface

DGET New Delhi and CSTARI Kolkata have been implementing an annual pattern for all businesses in ITI since the August 2018 session. The examination system will also be changed and it will be online from this year and since all the questions are of Objective Type (MCQ), the trainees are in dire need of in-depth study. It is with this in mind that we are delighted to present the books based on the old NIMI pattern and a complete overview of the new annual pattern, and we hope that these books will be a guide for all business directors and trainees. Is.

For writing these books, Johar Awate Saheb, Principal of ITI Akluj. Former Principal of ITI Satara Saigavkar Saheb, Assistant Director Shri Chandrakant Dhekne Saheb Regional Office of Vocational Education and Training, Pune, District Vocational Education and Training Officer Sachin Dhumal Saheb and Headmaster Government Technical School Kendra Shalmali Pawar Madam and son Adhiraj Dole, mother Kusum Dole, I am very grateful to my father Madhukar Dole and wife Ashwini Dole for their special guidance and cooperation from time to time.

Also, in a very short period of time, the book was reviewed by Shri Rajendra Ghume Saheb, Joint Director, Vocational Education and Training Regional Office, Pune, for his invaluable time in publishing the book. I am sincerely grateful for their feedback.

I am grateful to the Instructor of ITI Satara for there continuous support from the very beginning of writing the book.

From this book, I consider myself blessed to have shared my thoughts on e-learning with you. I will not claim that this book is perfect, because considering the perfection, this book is an attempt and is in its infancy. They will be valuable for improvement if they are tested and suggested.

Manoj Dole
Dated 9/1/2019

Acknowledgements

The industrial training and theoretical examination system of our industrial training institutes and these changes have been accepted by the craft instructors and the trainees. Theoretical examinations conducted in your industrial training institutes are also conducted online. Since these examinations are of multiple choice MCQ method, the trainees will need to get more practice of such questions.

With all these considerations in mind, Mr. Manoj Madhukar, Director, Dole Crafts, Katari Industrial Training Institute, Satara, has done a thorough study and with his diligent work and added his keen intellect, according to the new annual system and NSQF-5 syllabus, e-book of Katari and other machine trades. -Book) and they have created mobile apps and blogs on theoretical topics to make training easier and have made all these educational materials available for download on the world famous websites Google Play Store, Amazon and Apple Book Store. Training has been made easier by creating a print version and using advanced techniques like QR Code.

All these educational materials will definitely be a guide for all the trainees for in-depth study and for the craft instructors and other concerned who are imparting vocational training.

CHAPTER ONE

Mechanic Motor Vehicle Second Year MCQ Drawing

Online Test Exam

ITI Books

CNC Course

AutoCAD CAM

JOB & Apprentice

Online Theory

Computer Course

Trading Course

Web Designing

MSCIT Course

Shopping Business

Internet Business

Remotasks Course

Online Services

Top Sportsmans

Indian Army

Freedom Fighters

Top Scientists

Social Reformers

Motivational Speaker

Top Richest People

Join WhatsApp Group

Join Facebook Group

Like Facebook Page

PAN / Adhar / Licence Passport

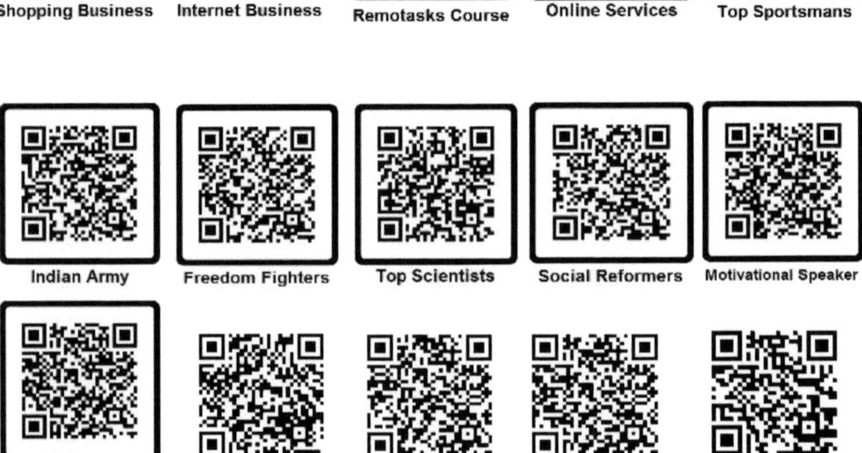

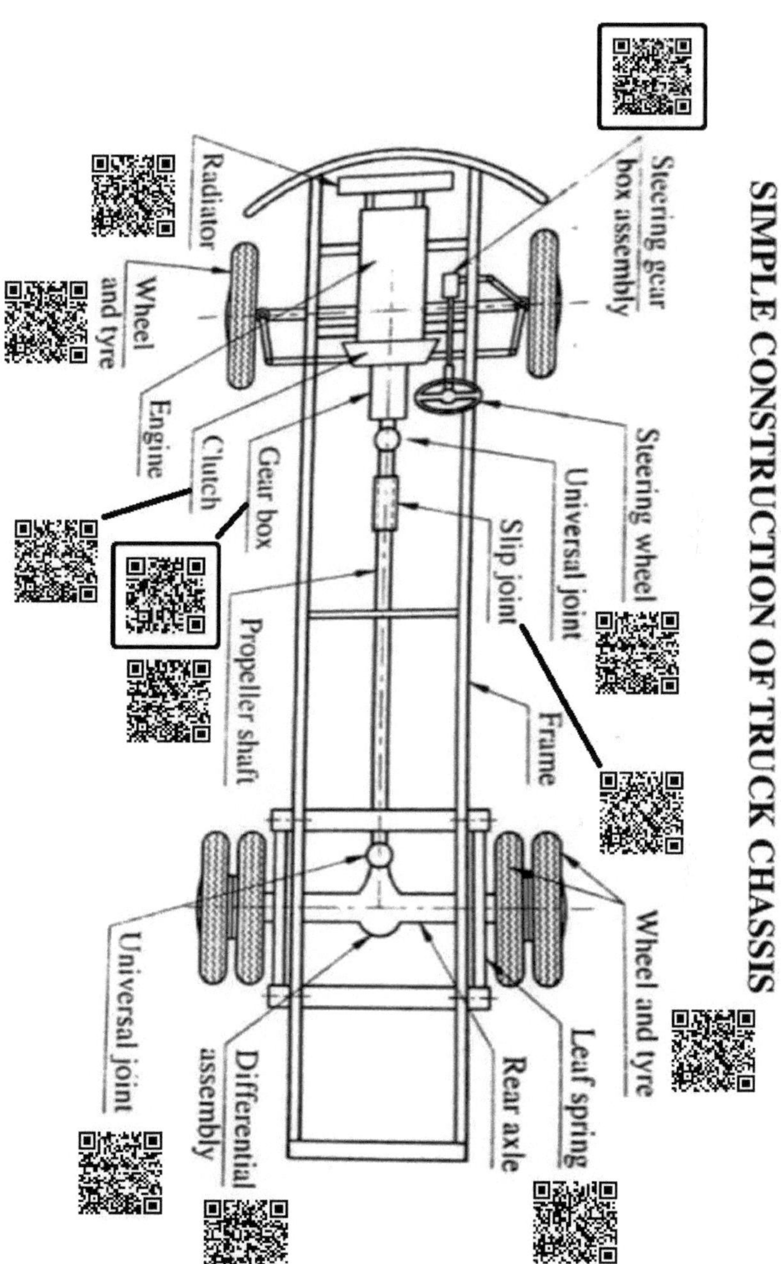
SIMPLE CONSTRUCTION OF TRUCK CHASSIS
Steering gear box assembly
Radiator
Wheel and tyre
Engine
Clutch
Gear box
Propeller shaft
Steering wheel
Universal joint
Slip joint
Frame
Wheel and tyre
Leaf spring
Rear axle
Differential assembly
Universal joint

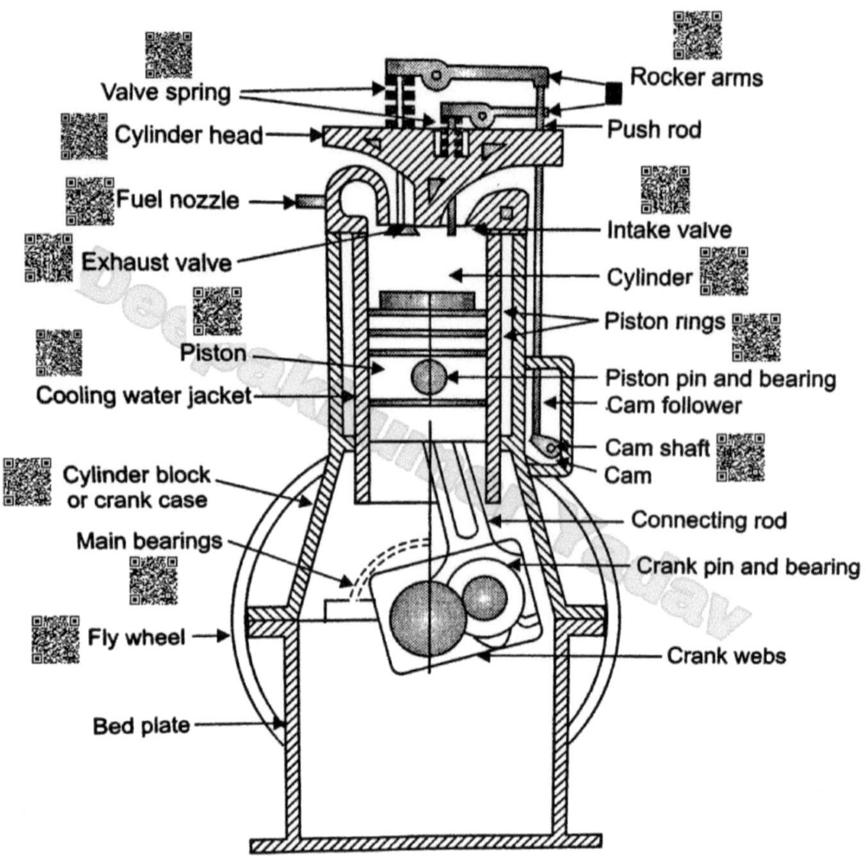

Components of Diesel Engine

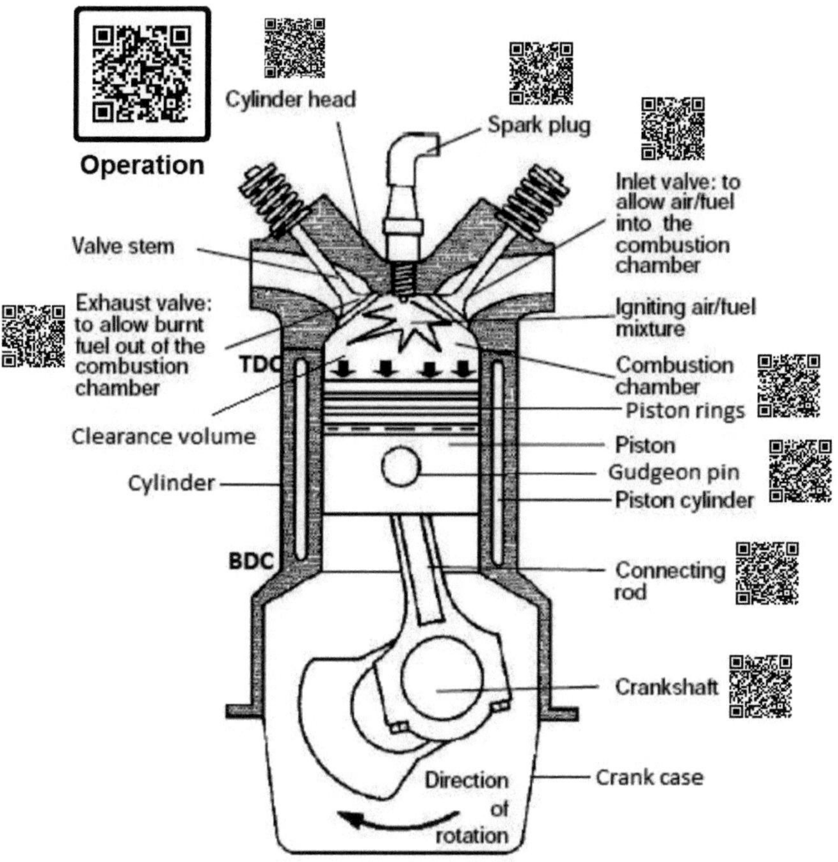

Petrol Engine Details

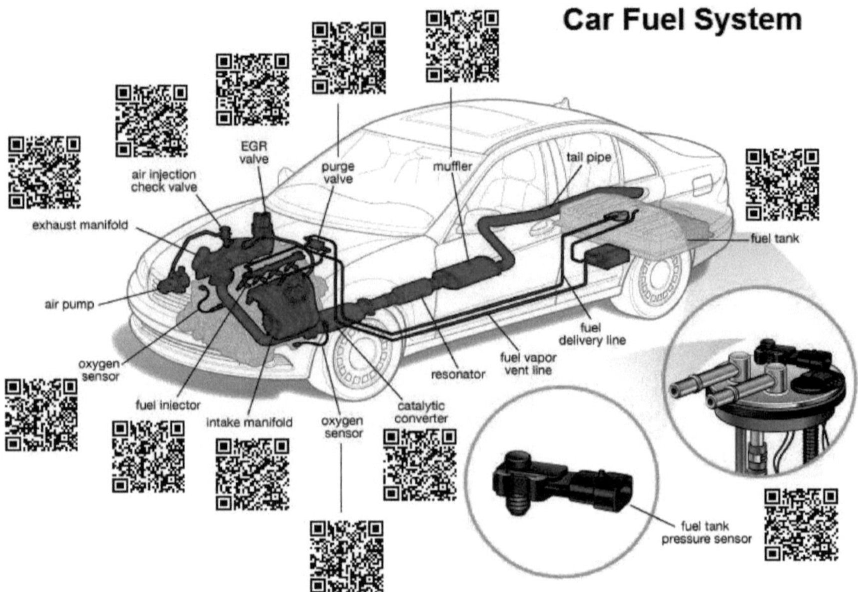
Car Fuel System
EGR valve
purge valve
muffler
tail pipe
air injection check valve
exhaust manifold
fuel tank
air pump
fuel delivery line
oxygen sensor
fuel vapor vent line
resonator
fuel injector
catalytic converter
intake manifold
oxygen sensor
fuel tank pressure sensor

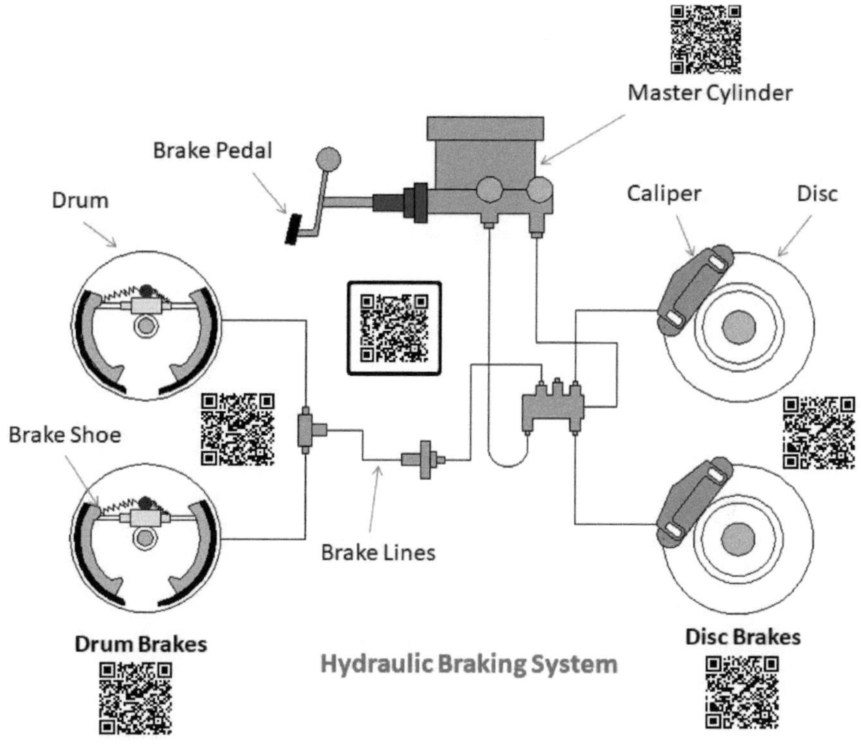

Multi Point Fuel Injection Syastem D- MPFI & L- MPFI

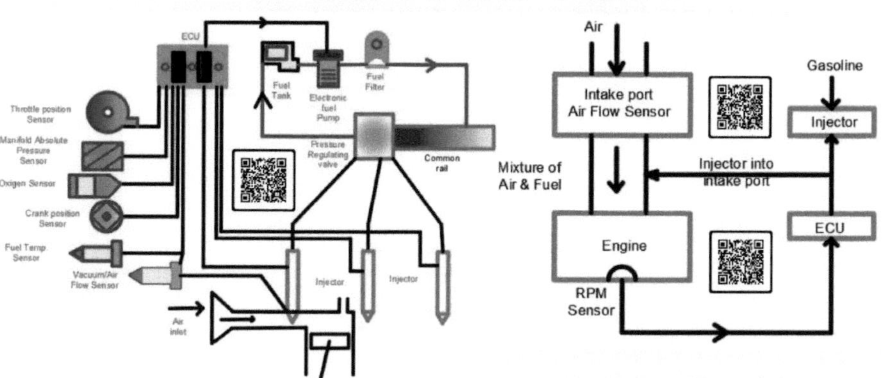

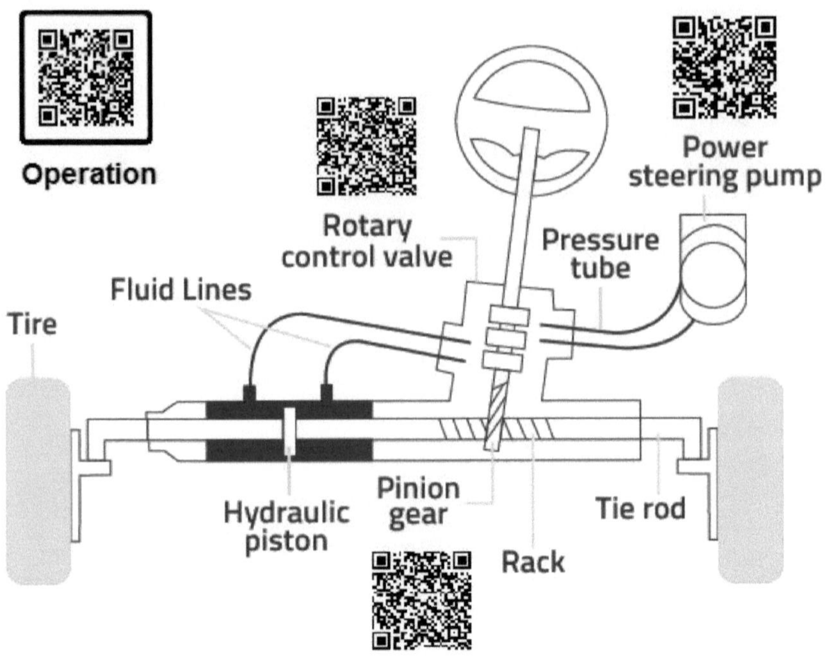

Power Steering System

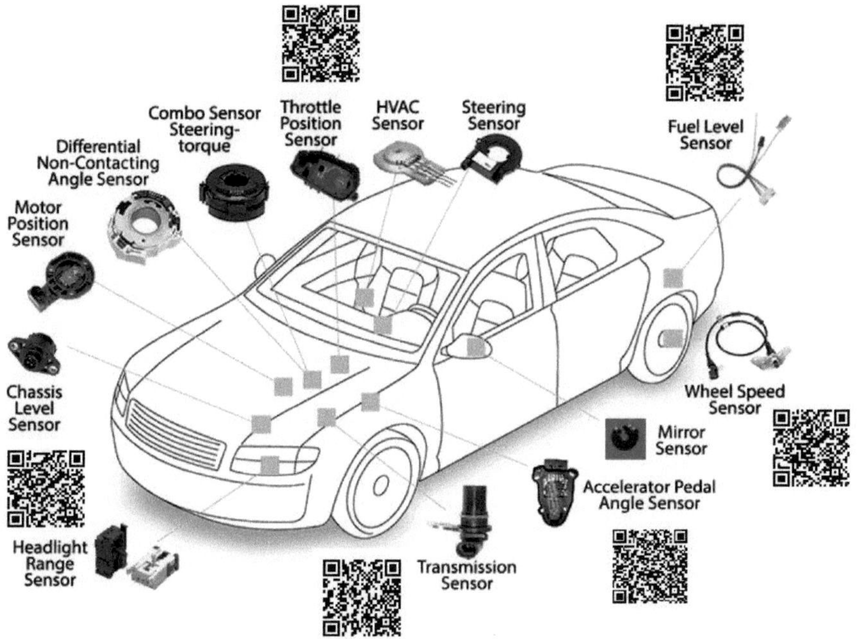

Car Sensor System

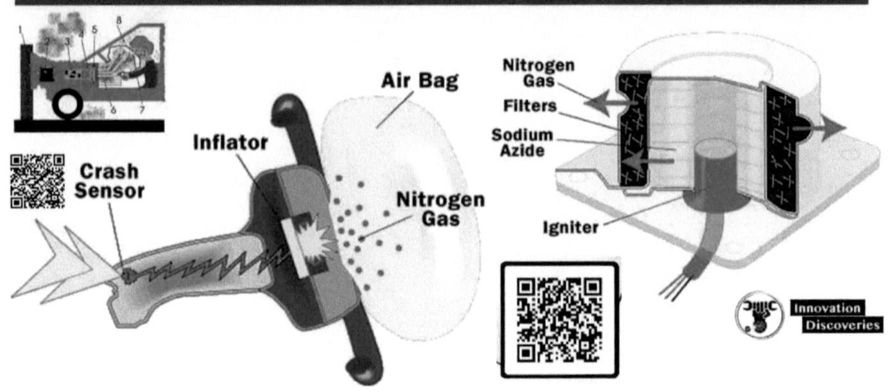
WHAT IS AIRBAG?
HOW IT WORKS DURING AN ACCIDENT?
Air Bag
Inflator
Crash
Sensor
Nitrogen
Gas
Nitrogen
Gas
Filters
Sodium
Azide
Igniter
Innovation
Discoveries

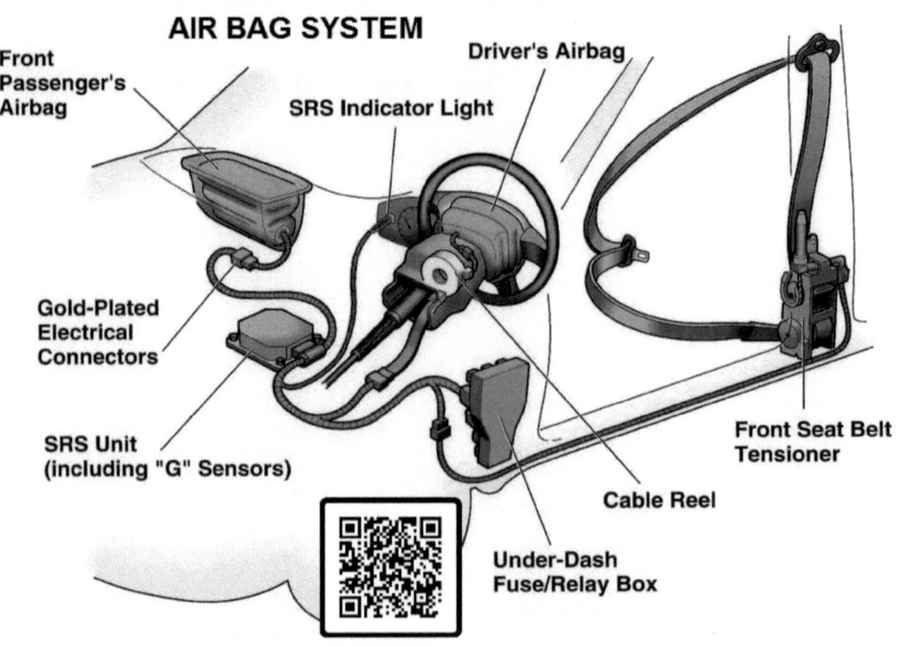
AIR BAG SYSTEM
Front
Passenger's
Airbag
Driver's Airbag
SRS Indicator Light
Gold-Plated
Electrical
Connectors
SRS Unit
(including "G" Sensors)
Front Seat Belt
Tensioner
Cable Reel
Under-Dash
Fuse/Relay Box

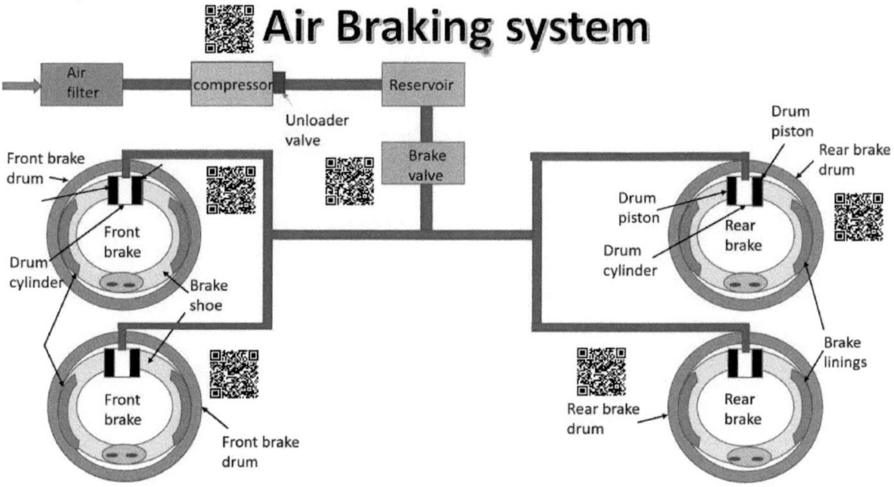

Air Braking system

Air filter
compressor
Reservoir
Unloader valve
Brake valve
Front brake drum
Front brake
Drum cylinder
Brake shoe
Front brake
Front brake drum
Drum piston
Rear brake drum
Drum piston
Rear brake
Drum cylinder
Brake linings
Rear brake drum
Rear brake

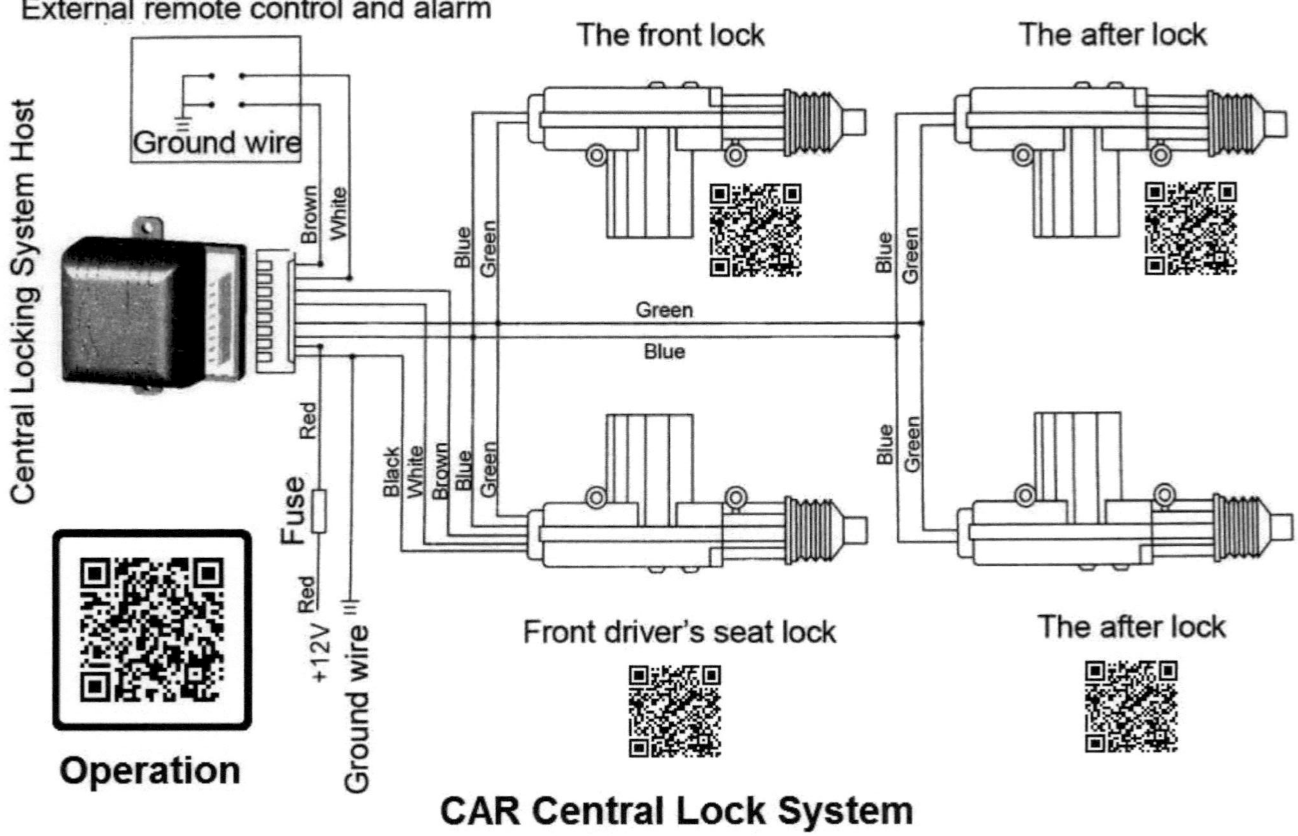
External remote control and alarm
Ground wire
Central Locking System Host
Brown
White
The front lock
The after lock
Blue
Green
Green
Blue
Red
Fuse
Red
+12V
Ground wire
Black
White
Brown
Blue
Green
Operation
Front driver's seat lock
The after lock
CAR Central Lock System

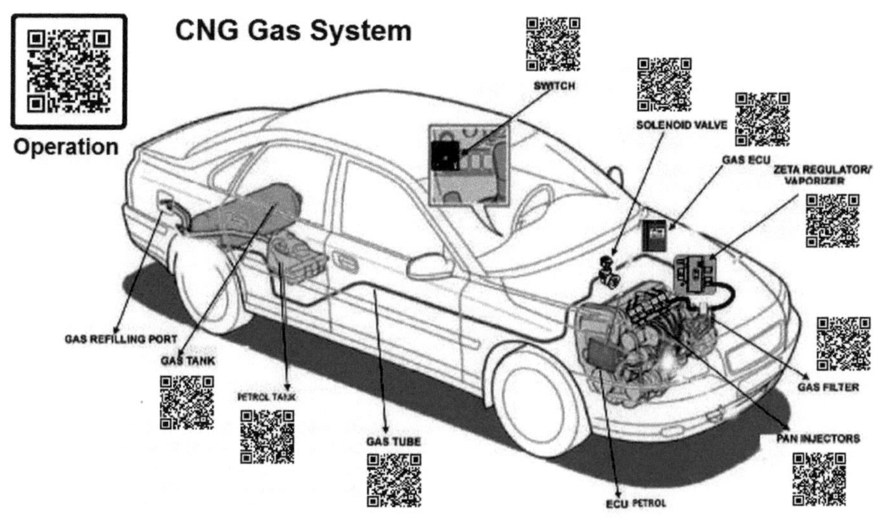
CNG Gas System
Operation
SWITCH
SOLENOID VALVE
GAS ECU
ZETA REGULATOR/ VAPORIZER
GAS REFILLING PORT
GAS TANK
PETROL TANK
GAS TUBE
GAS FILTER
PAN INJECTORS
ECU PETROL

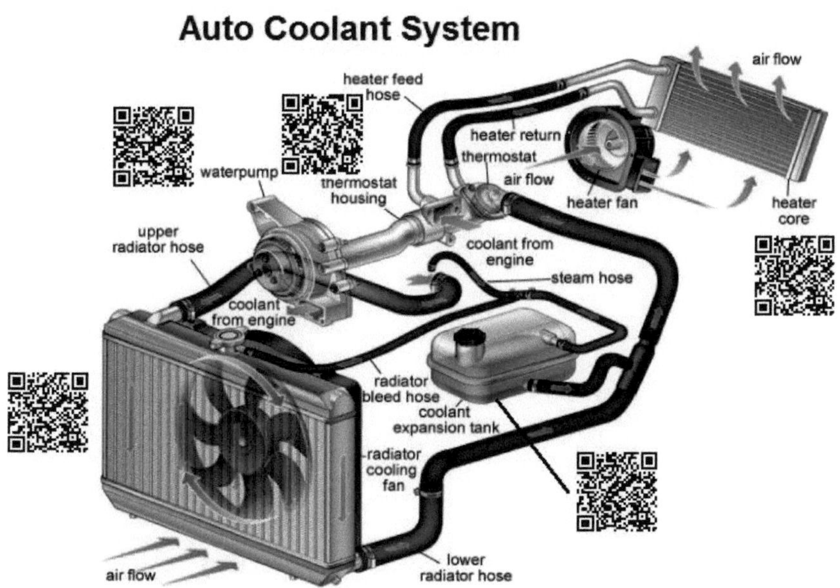
Auto Coolant System
heater feed hose
air flow
heater return
thermostat
air flow
waterpump
thermostat housing
heater fan
heater core
upper radiator hose
coolant from engine
steam hose
coolant from engine
radiator bleed hose
coolant expansion tank
radiator cooling fan
air flow
lower radiator hose

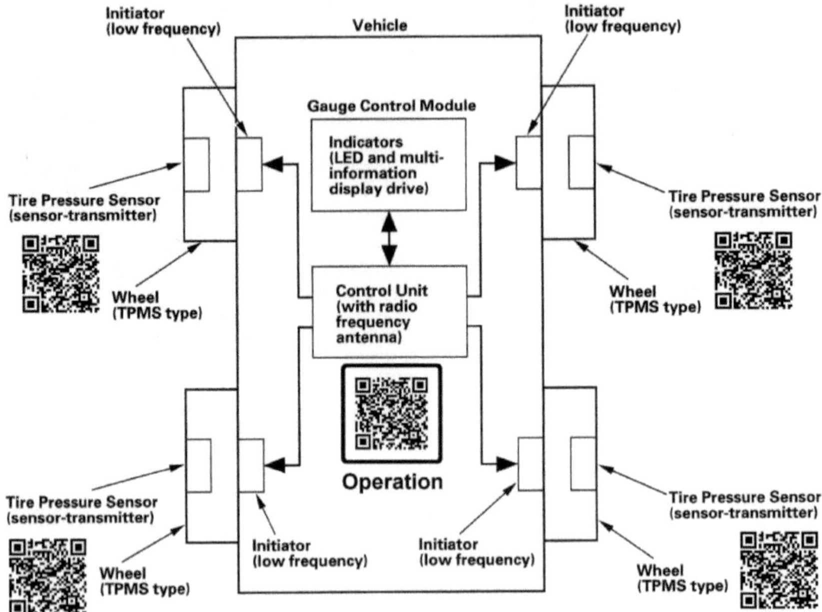

Car Tire Pressure Monitoring System (TPMS)

CHAPTER TWO

Mechanic Motor Vehicle Second Year MCQ

1] Disconnects engine for gear change

A] Engine

B] Clutches

C] Final drive

D] U joints

2] Pulls out pressure plate.

A] Clutch cover

B] Release bearing

C] Release fingers

D] Clutch plate

3] Transmits engine torque to transmission shaft.

A] Clutch cover

B] Release bearing

C] Release fingers

D] Clutch plate

4] Pushes with drawl plate

A] Clutch cover

B] Release bearing

C] Release fingers

D] Clutch plate

5] Holds pressure plate with fly wheel

A] Clutch cover

B] Release bearing

C] Release fingers

D] Clutch plate

6] Used in gear box

A] Multi plate clutch
B] Dog clutch
C] Cone clutch
D] Diaphragm clutch

Dog clutches in vehicle

7] provides more frictional area
A] Multi plate clutch
B] Dog clutch
C] Cone clutch
D] Diaphragm clutch
8] smaller flywheel is used
A] Multi plate clutch
B] Dog clutch
C] Cone clutch
D] Diaphragm clutch
9] Spring acts as a release lever
A] Multi plate clutch
B] Dog clutch
C] Cone clutch
D] Diaphragm clutch
10] Type of drive mechanism
A] Pinion
B] Over running clutch
C] Plunger disk
D] Clutch
11] Prevents over speeding of pinion and armature
A] Pinion
B] Over running clutch
C] Plunger disk
D] Clutch

12] Engages with the flywheel ring

A] Pinion

B] Over running clutch

C] Plunger disk

D] Clutch

13] Connect two terminals of solenoid.

A] Pinion

B] Over running clutch

C] Plunger disk

D] Clutch

14] Double declutch IS not necessary

A] Sliding mesh

B] Synchromesh

C] Double declutching

D] Transfer case

15] Used in four-wheel drive vehicle

A] Sliding mesh

B] Synchromesh

C] Double declutching

D] Transfer case

16] Only spur gears are used

A] Sliding mesh

B] Synchromesh

C] Double declutching

D] Transfer case

17] Used for smooth gear shifting

A] Sliding mesh

B] Synchromesh

C] Double declutching

D] Transfer case

18] Hard gear shifting is due to

A] Worn out clutch disc

B] Damaged main shaft bearings

C] Synchronizer unit damaged

D] excessive oil in the gearbox.

Gear

19] Gear slip is due to

A] Worn out synchroniser

B] Worn out clutch disc

C] Dry main shaft bearing

D] Weak pressure spring of clutch.

20] Noise in particular gear is due to

A] Insufficient clutch pedal free play

B] Damage gear teeth

C] Cracked gear box case

D] Damaged synchromesh unit.

21] While reversing the vehicle the driver should control

A] Clutch

B] Forward gear

C] Accelerator

D] Hand brake.

22] The clutch plate assembly has a centre steel disc riveted with springs for

A] strength

B] flexibility

C] less noise

D] absorbing shocks

23] Dog clutches are used in

A] gear boxes

B] friction clutches

C] brakes

D] differentials

Speed gear box in vehicle

24] Synchromesh mechanisms is provided for

A] Increasing the speed of the vehicle

B] Reducing the speed of the vehicle

C] Smooth gear engagement'

D] None of the above.

25] Only spur gears are used

A] Sliding mesh

B] Synchromesh

C] Double declutching

D] Transfer case

26] Used for smooth gear shifting

A] Sliding mesh

B] Synchromesh

C] Double declutching

D] Transfer case

27] Hard gear shifting is due to

A] Worn out clutch disc

B] Damaged main shaft bearings

C] Synchronizer unit damaged

D] Excessive oil in the gearbox.

28] Gear slip is due to

A] Worn out synchroniser

B] Worn out clutch disc

C] Dry main shaft bearing

D] Weak pressure spring of clutch.

29] Noise in particular gear is due to

A] Insufficient clutch pedal free play

B] Damage gear teeth

C] Cracked gear box case

D] Damaged synchromesh unit.

30] Gearshift lever is used for

A] Releasing clutch

B] Changing gear

C] Increasing the speed of the engine

D] Controlling the direction of vehicle.

31] In which type of steering gear box variable steering ration is achieved?

A] worm and roller steering gear

B] worm and nut steering gear

C] worm and sector steering gear

D] rack and pinion steering gear

Steering gearbox in vehicle

32] The vehicle attains different speed by means of

A] gear box

B] clutch

C] differential

D] rear axle & wheel

33] Dog clutches are used in

A] gear boxes

B] friction clutches

C] brakes

D] differentials

34] in a 3 speed gear box in following combination of gears are provided

A] 3 forward and 1 reverse

B] 2 forward and 1 reverse

C] 4 forward

D] 2 forward and 2 reverse

35] which gear does not produce axial trust

A] spur gear

B] helical gear

C] spiral bevel gear

D] bevel gear

36] which gears converts rotary motion into linear motion

A] worm gears

B] herring bone gear

C] rack & pinion

D] helical gear

37] What is a reason for gear slip

A] unlubricated gear linka-ges

B] less oil in gear box

C] broken teeth of gear

D] wrong adjustment of gear lever

38] In a differential gear ratio can be calculated from any one of the following statements

A] sun gear

B] planetary gear

C] crown wheel

D] pinion

Differential gear box in truck

39] low engine oil pressure may be due to

A] clogged oil filter

B] more oil filled in the oil sump

C] high viscosity of oil used

D] excessive backlash between pump gears

40] Increases road wheel torque

A] Engine

B] Clutches

C] Final drive

D] U joints

41] Used in four-wheel drive vehicle

A] Sliding mesh

B] Synchromesh

C] Double declutching

D] Transfer case

42] Four wheel drive should be used

A] Always

B] While climbing up hill

C] On sand (slushy ground)
D] While climbing down hill.
43] While driving in a wet or sandy roads always use
A] Four wheel drive only
B] Two wheel drive only
C] First gear only
D] More acceleration.
44] Fluid under pressures
A] To start heavy duty engine
B] Starter motor
C] Hydraulic cranking
D] Electric motor
45] Gasoline engine
A] To start heavy duty engine
B] Starter motor
C] Hydraulic cranking
D] Electric motor
46] Battery power
A] To start heavy duty engine
B] Starter motor
C] Hydraulic cranking
D] Electric motor
47] Air compressor's driven by
A] To start heavy duty engine
B] Starter motor
C] Hydraulic cranking
D] Electric motor
48] Hydraulic floor jack is used
A] To remove king pin bush
B] To lift the wheel
C] To press the bush
D] Hold the job.
49]The pressure of fluid in hydraulic brake system is governed by
A] boils law
B] Charles law
C] Pascal's law
D] none of the above laws
50] the fluid pressure in master cylinder depends on

A] master cylinder piston area
B] wheel cylinder piston area
C] pipe line dia
D] fluid viscosity
51] Allows fluid both way in and out of cylinder
A] Piston
B] Push Rod
C] Primary cup
D] Check valve
52] Seals the compensating port
A] Piston
B] Push Rod
C] Primary cup
D] Check valve
53] Actuates the piston
A] Piston
B] Push Rod
C] Primary cup
D] Check valve
54] Develops pressure on fluid
A] Piston
B] Push Rod
C] Primary cup
D] Check valve

55] Develops pressure on fuel to go out
A] Valves
B] Coil spring
C] Diaphragm
D] Rocker arm
56] Actuates the diaphragm
A] Valves
B] Coil spring
C] Diaphragm
D] Rocker arm
57] Allow fuel to flow in and out
A] Valves
B] Coil spring
C] Diaphragm
D] Rocker arm

Engine valves

58] Helps to return the diaphragm.

A] Valves

B] Coil spring

C] Diaphragm

D] Rocker arm

59] An overflow valve is used

A] to send back excess fuel from the fuel filler

B] to supply more fuel to the fuel filter

C] to supply clean fuel

D] to take the leaking fuel.

60] Excessive oil pressure in the lubrication system may be due to

A] less quantity of engine oil in sump

B] incorrect adjustment of relief valve

C] less suction effect on the suction pipe

D] none of the above

61] when oil pressure increases above set limit, oil returns to sump through

A] pressure relief valve

B] by pass valve

C] oil filter

D] oil pump

62] Helps to turn the stub axles

A] Front axle

B] Track rod

C] Stub axle

D] Stub axle arm

63] Carries springs and steering linkages.

A] Front axle

B] Track rod

C] Stub axle

D] Stub axle arm

64] Transmits steering wheel movement to stub axle

A] Front axle

B] Track rod

C] Stub axle

D] Stub axle arm

65] Pivots about king pin for steering purpose

A] Front axle

B] Track rod

C] Stub axle
D] Stub axle arm
66] Acts as a seat for spring mounting
A] Kingpin
B] Spring pad
C] Stub axle shaft portion
D] Track rod ball joints
67] Connects front axle with stub axle
A] Kingpin
B] Spring pad
C] Stub axle shaft portion
D] Track rod ball joints
68] Provides flexible movement for track rod
A] Kingpin
B] Spring pad
C] Stub axle shaft portion
D] Track rod ball joints
69] Accommodates wheel hub bearings.
A] Kingpin
B] Spring pad
C] Stub axle shaft portion
D] Track rod ball joints
70] Pivots on the bottom of frame and acts as a seat for spring
A] Upper control arm
B] Coil spring
C] Ball joints
D] Lower control arm
71] Acts as pivot for steering knuckle movement
A] Upper control arm
B] Coil spring
C] Ball joints
D] Lower control arm
72] Provides cushioning effect
A] Upper control arm
B] Coil spring
C] Ball joints
D] Lower control arm
73] Pivots on the top of frame and acts as a seat for spring

A] Upper control arm

B] Coil spring

C] Ball joints

D] Lower control arm

74] When front wheels are in straight ahead position and lines are drawn through king pins centre and steering arms end, at which point they will meet?

A] At centre of front axle

B] At centre of chassis

C] At centre of rear axle behind differential

D] At centre of rear axle just ahead of differential

75] Transmits its motion to meshing parts

A] Steering wheel

B] Worm

C] Steering column

D] Sector/roller/ball nut/peg

76] Rotates the steering column

A] Steering wheel

B] Worm

C] Steering column

D] Sector/roller/ball nut/peg

77] Rotates in an arc movement and transmits it to cross shaft

A] Steering wheel

B] Worm

C] Steering column

D] Sector/roller/ball nut/peg

78] Rotates the worm

A] Steering wheel

B] Worm

C] Steering column

D] Sector/roller/ball

79] Outward tilt of front wheel

A] Negative camber angle

B] Positive caster angle

C] Kingpin inclination

D] Included angle vehicle

80] Inward tilt of front wheel

A] Negative camber angle

B] Positive caster angle

C] Kingpin inclination

D] Included angle vehicle

81] The angle between tyre centre line and kingpin centre line

A] Negative camber angle

B] Positive caster angle

C] Kingpin inclination

D] Included angle vehicle

82] Tilt of kingpin towards centre of vehicle

A] Negative camber angle

B] Positive caster angle

C] Kingpin inclination

D] Included angle vehicle

83] In which type of steering gear box variable steering ration is achieved?

A] worm and roller steering gear

B] worm and nut steering gear

C] worm and sector steering gear

D] rack and pinion steering gear

84] A strut rod in a suspension is used in

A] conventional I beam axle type suspension

B] coil spring type suspension system

C] torsion bar suspension system

D] Macpherson system

85] Carries springs and steering linkages.

A] Front axle

B] Track rod

C] Stub axle

D] Stub axle arm

86] Acts as a seat for spring mounting

A] Kingpin

B] Spring pad

C] Stub axle shaft portion

D] Track rod ball joints

87] Pivots on the bottom of frame and acts as a seat for spring

A] Upper control arm

B] Coil spring

C] Ball joints

D] Lower control arm

88] Provides cushioning effect

A] Upper control arm

B] Coil spring

C] Ball joints

D] Lower control arm

89] in a Hotchkiss drive rear and driving torque is taken up by

A] rear axle housing

B] rear leaf spring

C] shock absorber

D] engine mountings

90] Helper spring is used in

A] Cars

B] jeep

C] light motor vehicle

D] heavy trucks

91] The angle between tyre centre line and kingpin centre line

A] Negative camber angle

B] Positive caster angle

C] Kingpin inclination

D] Included angle vehicle

92] Bald spots appearing on tyre's outer surface is due to

A] Excessive speed

B] lack of rotation of tyres

C] unbalanced wheel

D] over inflation

93] The angle between centre line of king pin and a vertical line from centre point of tyre is called

A. camber angle

B. caster angle

C. toe out angle on turns

D. kingpin inclination

94] Brings back the pedal to normal position

A] Brake pedal

B] Linkage

C] Cam

D] Pedal return spring

95] Expands the brake shoe

A] Brake pedal
B] Linkage
C] Cam
D] Pedal return spring
96] Operates the cam
A] Brake pedal
B] Linkage
C] Cam
D] Pedal return spring
97] Operates the linkages
A] Brake pedal
B] Linkage
C] Cam
D] Pedal return spring
98] Supplies fluid to front and rear wheels
A] Brake pedal
B] Master cylinder piston
C] Wheel cylinder piston
D] Distribution block
99] Pushes the brake shoe towards drum
A] Brake pedal
B] Master cylinder piston
C] Wheel cylinder piston
D] Distribution block
100] Creates pressure on fluid
A] Brake pedal
B] Master cylinder piston
C] Wheel cylinder piston
D] Distribution block
101] Pushes master cylinder piston through linkages.
A] Brake pedal
B] Master cylinder piston
C] Wheel cylinder piston
D] Distribution block
102] Allows fluid both way in and out of cylinder
A] Piston
B] Push Rod
C] Primary cup

D] Check valve

103] Seals the compensating port

A] Piston

B] Push Rod

C] Primary cup

D] Check valve

104] Actuates the piston

A] Piston

B] Push Rod

C] Primary cup

D] Check valve

105] Develops pressure on fluid

A] Piston

B] Push Rod

C] Primary cup

D] Check valve

106] Among the following which material is not used for brake drum.

A] Steel

B] Copper

C] Cast iron

D] Aluminium alloy

107] The purpose of using a rubber boot at the ends of a wheel cylinder is...

A] to prevent entry of foreign particles

B] to allow air inside the cylinder

C] to allow return brake fluid to leak out

D] to stop exit of air from the cylinder

108] To reduce noise during reverse braking

A] Double piston wheel cylinder

B] Single piston wheel cylinder

C] Step-bore wheel cylinder

D] Baffle type wheel cylinders

109] To increase braking force on shoes

A] Double piston wheel cylinder

B] Single piston wheel cylinder

C] Step-bore wheel cylinder

D] Baffle type wheel cylinders

110] For operating two leading shoe brakes

A] Double piston wheel cylinder
B] Single piston wheel cylinder
C] Step-bore wheel cylinder
D] Baffle type wheel cylinders
111] For operating leading and trailing shoe brakes
A] Double piston wheel cylinder
B] Single piston wheel cylinder
C] Step-bore wheel cylinder
D] Baffle type wheel cylinders

Air tank safety valve

112] Relieves excess pressure of air from the air tank.
A] Air compressor
B] Unloader valve
C] Safety valve
D] Brake chamber

Brakes in car

113] Houses diaphragm and pushrod
A] Air compressor

B] Unloader valve
C] Safety valve
D] Brake chamber

114] Provides compressed air to system
A] Air compressor
B] Unloader valve
C] Safety valve
D] Brake chamber

115] Regulates maximum air pressure, reaching to air tank.
A] Air compressor
B] Unloader valve
C] Safety valve
D] Brake chamber

116] How brakes are applied in fail safe brake system during parking
A] by air pressure in brake actuator
B] By spring pressure in brake actuator
C] by vacuum in brake actuator
D] by mechanical hand brake

117] Supplies air to front and rear brake
A] Brake actuator
B] Dual brake valve
C] System protection valve
D] Flick valve

118] Operated for parking the vehicle.
A] Brake actuator
B] Dual brake valve
C] System protection valve
D] Flick valve

119] Exerts spring pressure and applies brake when air pressure in system is less
A] Brake actuator
B] Dual brake valve
C] System protection valve
D] Flick valve

120] Distributes air to various circuits
A] Brake actuator
B] Dual brake valve
C] System protection valve

D] Flick valve

121] To indicate the vehicle is being braked

A] Headlight

B] Parking light

C] Stop light

122] Used as no plate lamp and brake lamp

B] Miniature bulb

C] Festoon bulb

D] S.C / S.F.

E] D.C/ D.F.

123] parkingbreakes are generally operated by

A] hand lever operation

B] brake pedal operation

C] electrical switch control operation

D] none of the above

124]The pressure of fluid in hydraulic brake system is governed by

A] boils law

B] Charles law

C] Pascal's law

D] none of the above laws

125] The fluid pressure in master cylinder depends on

A] master cylinder piston area

B] wheel cylinder piston area

C] pipe line dia

D] fluid viscosity

126] the tandem master has

A] two reservoirs and two outlets

B] one reservoir and two outlets

C] tow reservoir and one outlet

D] one reservoir and one outlet

127] Which defects of brake drum cannot be corrected by turning?

A] taper

B] over heating

C] ovality

D] scoring

128]The fluid pressure in a wheel cylinder can be increased by any one of the following methods

A] by changing dia of piston

B] by changing dia of rubber cup
C] by changing the spring
D] by interchanging of brake shoes
129] Air tank is made of
A]steel
B] copper
C] plastic
D] brass
130] Safety valve on air tank prevents
A] oil accumulation in air tank
B] excess air reaching to brake valve
C] bursting of air tank at high pressure
D] vehicle to move when brake has failed
131] How many air tanks are used in dual air brake system
A] one
B] two
C] three
D] four
132] Person acts as a steerman of the vehicle is called
A] conductor
B] Driver
C] Passenger
D] spectator.
133] Act for leaving the vehicle in dangerous position
A] 125 of MV ACT 1988
B] 126 of MV ACT 1988
C] 128 of MV ACT 1988
D] 122 of MV ACT 1988
134] Act for Riding on running board
B] 126 of MV ACT 1988
C] 128 of MV ACT 1988
D] 122 of MV ACT 1988
E] 123 of MV ACT 1988
135] Act for Obstruction of driver
A] 125 of MV ACT 1988
B] 126 of MV ACT 1988
C] 128 of MV ACT 1988
D] 122 of MV ACT 1988

136] Act for Stationary vehicles
A] 125 of MV ACT 1988
B] <u>126 of MV ACT 1988</u>
C] 128 of MV ACT 1988
D] 122 of MV ACT 1988
137] Act for Safety measures for drivers and pillion riders
A] 125 of MV ACT 1988
B] 126 of MV ACT 1988
C] <u>128 of MV ACT 1988</u>
D] 122 of MV ACT 1988
138] Carries fuel
A] Carburettor
B] Pump
C] Pipe lines
D] <u>Petrol tank</u>
139] Stores petrol
A] Carburettor
B] Pump
C] Pipe lines
D] <u>Petrol tank</u>
140] Delivers petrol to the engine
A] <u>Carburettor</u>
B] Pump
C] Pipe lines
D] Petrol tank
141] Delivers petrol to carburettor
A] Carburettor
B] <u>Pump</u>
C] Pipe lines
D] Petrol tank
142] Holds petrol
A] Air horn
B] <u>Fuel bowl</u>
C] Air cleaner
D] Air bleed
143] if petrol air mixture is compressed in a cylinder
A] its volume reduces
B] its pressure will rise

C] its temperature will increase
D] all the above will happen
144]During suction stroke the charge drawn in a petrol engine is
A] air only
B. air and petrol mixture
C] petrol only
D] fuels other than petrol

Petrol engine in car

145] In a petrol engine air fuel mixture is drawn into the cylinder due to vacuum created during
A] power stroke
B] exhaust stroke
C] suction stroke
D] compression stroke
146] the high fuel consumption of a petrol engine may be due to
A] leakage of fuel from carburetor
B] defects in lubrication system
C] air leaks in intake manifold
D] incorrect idle speed (too low)
147] the float circuit is provided in a carburetor
A] to store fuel vapours
B] to supply mixture of air & fuel
C] to maintain proper level of fuel in float chamber
D] none of the above
148] increase or decrease the speed of the engine
B] Speedometer

C] Clutch pedal
D] Ignition switch
E] Accelerator

Engine in vehicle

149] While allowing other vehicle to overtake
A] Accelerate
B] Reduce accelerator
C] Stop the vehicle
D] Move the vehicle to right.

150] Fuel catching fire
A] T.D.C.
B] Cycle
C] B.D.C.
D] Ignition
151] To seal the tank externally.
A] Baffles
B] Filter cap
C] Passage in the baffle
D] Filler neck
152] Prevents slashing of fuel in the tank
A] Baffles
B] Filter cap
C] Passage in the baffle
D] Filler neck
153] To fill fuel in the tank
A] Baffles
B] Filter cap
C] Passage in the baffle
D] Filler neck
154] To transfer fuel from one compartment to other compartment
A] Baffles
B] Filter cap
C] Passage in the baffle
D] Filler neck
155] Carries fuel
A] Carburettor
B] Pump
C] Pipe lines
D] Petrol tank
156] Stores petrol
A] Carburettor
B] Pump
C] Pipe lines
D] Petrol tank
157] Delivers diesel to the engine
A] Carburettor
B] Pump

C] Pipe lines
D] Petrol tank
158] Delivers diesel to carburettor
A] Carburettor
B] Pump
C] Pipe lines
D] Petrol tank

Fuel pump in Vehicle

159] Holds diesel
A] Air horn
B] Fuel bowl
C] Air cleaner
D] Air bleed
160] Serves as passage for air
A] Air horn
B] Fuel bowl
C] Air cleaner

D] Air bleed
161] Helps in breaking up fuel particles
A] Air horn
B] Fuel bowl
C] Air cleaner
D] Air bleed
162] Cleans the air entering the cylinder
A] Air horn
B] Fuel bowl
C] Air cleaner
D] Air bleed
163] Develops pressure on fuel to go out
A] Valves
B] Coil spring
C] Diaphragm
D] Rocker arm
164] Actuates the diaphragm
A] Valves
B] Coil spring
C] Diaphragm
D] Rocker arm
165] Allow fuel to flow in and out
A] Valves
B] Coil spring
C] Diaphragm
D] Rocker arm
166] When the engine temperature is high, the resistance in the engine unit becomes
A] less
B] More
C] remains constant
D] Fluctuates.
167] The actuating wire is made of
A] lead
B] Aluminium
C] Copper
D] nichrome
168] When the iron core turns to magnet it attracts

A] Main armature
B] Auxiliary armature
C] Both the armature
D] No armature.
169] Flasher unit terminals are marked as
A] HBS
B] LBP
C] ISB
D] ABF
170] Separates the points
A] Solenoid Switch
B] Actuating wire (when heated)
C] Ballast Resistors
D] Actuating wire (when cooled)
171] Limits the current to the points
A] Solenoid Switch
B] Actuating wire (when heated)
C] Ballast Resistors
D] Actuating wire (when cooled)
172] Closes the points
A] Solenoid Switch
B] Actuating wire (when heated)
C] Ballast Resistors
D] Actuating wire (when cooled)
173] Turns core to magnet
A] Solenoid Switch
B] Actuating wire (when heated)
C] Ballast Resistors
D] Actuating wire (when cooled)
174] Flywheel magneto consists of
A] Temporary magnet
B] Bar magnet
C] Permanent magnet
D] Needle magnet.
175] in flywheel magneto, the ignition coil is
A] stationary
B] Moving
C] Rotating

D] Oscillating.

176] To prevent arcing in the points

A] Switch

B] Secondary coils

C] Flywheels

D] Condensers

177] To complete primary circuit

A] Switch

B] Secondary coils

C] Flywheels

D] Condensers

178] To induce H.T. current

A] Switch

B] Secondary coils

C] Flywheels

D] Condensers

179] To rotate the permanent magnet

A] Switch

B] Secondary coils

C] Flywheels

D] Condensers

180] When the engine rotates the current is first produced in the

A] Secondary winding

B] Primary winding

C] Both the coil

D] Condenser

181] The C.B. points open due to rotation of

A] armature

B] Cam

C] Flywheel

D] Magnet.

182] Stores current and reverses the same

A] Armature

B] Spark plug

C] Condenser

D] Horse shoe

183] Produces magnetic field

A] Armature

B] Spark plug
C] Condenser
D] Horse shoe
184] Opens the contact breaker points
B] Spark plug
C] Condenser
D] Horse shoe
E] Cam
185] Rotates between magnetic poles
A] Armature
B] Spark plug
C] Condenser
D] Horse shoe
186] Converts H.T. current to spark.
A] Armature
B] Spark plug
C] Condenser
D] Horse shoe
187] The alternators are used in the vehicles to
A] Charge the battery
B] Measure current
C] Measure voltage
D] Discharge battery.

Dynamo (Alternator) distributor cap in car

188] The A.C. current of alternator win be converted to D.C by using
A] condenser
B] Rectifier
C] Brushes
D] Induction coil.
189] The carbon brushes ride on the
A] Commutator
B] Armature
C] Slip ring
D] Rotor.
190] The ends of stator winding attached to the
A] Field coil
B] Carbon brush
C] Copper brush
D] Diodes.
191] Consists no of coils in slot

A] Diode
B] Stator
C] Fingers
D] Heat sink
192] Forms ‘S’& N poles
A] Diode
B] Stator
C] Fingers
D] Heat sink
193] Reads charging rate
B] Stator
C] Fingers
D] Heat sink
E] Ammeter
194] Absorbs the heat in diodes
A] Diode
B] Stator
C] Fingers
D] Heat sink
195] Made of silicon
A] Diode
B] Stator
C] Fingers
D] Heat sink
196] While fitting battery observe correct
A] Polarity
B] Mounting
C] Distilled water
D] Nothing
197] The output of the alternator is checked by
A] Flashing the leads
B] Looking
C] Using Instruments
D] Removing leads
198] Measures cell voltage
A] Resistance
B] Voltmeter
C] Ammeter

D] <u>Cell tester</u>

Lead acid battery in vehicle

199] Measures voltage of battery

A] Resistance

B] <u>Voltmeter</u>

C] Ammeter

D] Cell tester

200] Ohms is unit for

A] <u>Resistance</u>

B] Voltmeter

C] Ammeter

D] Cell tester

201] Fitted on panel board

A] Resistance

B] Voltmeter

C] <u>Ammeter</u>

D] Cell tester

202] If the thin cables are used for starter motor

A] <u>Cable wilt get heated up</u>

B] Voltage drop

C] Supply lesser current

D] Supply more current.

Starter winding armature in vehicle

203] The main feed wires from the battery consists the main colour of

A] White

B] Brown.

D] red

D] `78`Black

204] Earth circuit colour

C] Blue/red

D] Red
E] Black
F] White
205] Front parking lamp colour
A] Brown
B] Yellow
C] Blue/red
D] Red
206] ignition circuit colour
C] Blue/red
D] Red
E] Black
F] White
207] Generating circuit colour
A] Brown
B] Yellow
C] Blue/red
D] Red
208] Head light circuit colour
A] Brown
B] Yellow
C] Blue/red
D] Red
209] Battery feed circuit colour
A] Brown
B] Yellow
C] Blue/red
D] Red
210] The movement of the slide arm of the tank unit changes as per
A] current
B] Speed
C] Fuel level
D] Oil level.
211] When the float rises above due to full tank than the resistance of the tank unit
A] Fluctuates
B] remains constant
C] Lowers.

D] <u>Raises.</u>
212] When the tank begins to empty the tank unit fioat
A] <u>Falls down</u>
B] Raise up
C] Vibrates
D] remains steady.
213] connect two terminals of solenoid.
A] Pinion
B] Over running clutch
C] <u>Plunger disk</u>
D] Clutch
214] The lamp switches are fitted on
A] Steering column
B] <u>Panel board</u>
C] Gearlever
D] Hand brake lever.
215] The lamps are protected from overloading by
A] Switch
B] <u>Fuse</u>
C] Holder
D] Harness
216] Used as two wheeler tail lamp
A] A symmetrical bulb
B] Miniature bulb
C] <u>Festoon bulb</u>
D] S.C/ S.F.
217] Used as panel instrument lamp
A] A symmetrical bulb
B] <u>Miniature bulb</u>
C] Festoon bulb
D] S.C.IS.F.
218] To hold the reflector in position
A] <u>Headlamp</u>
B] Reflector
C] Lens
D] Adopter
219] Front parking lamp colour
A] Brown

B] Yellow
C] Blue/red
D] Red
220] The bulb filament is in the form of
A] Spiral
B] Straight
C] Loop
D] Star.
221] Used as headlight bulb
A] A symmetrical bulb
B] Miniature bulb
C] Festoon bulb
D] S.C.IS.F.
222] The head light parts can be replaced in
A] Sealed beam
B] Flush fitting type
C] refocused bulb
D] Halogen bulbs.
223] The head light is also used as
A] Side indicator
B] Stop indicator
C] Signalling device
D] Heating device.
224] To direct the shell light rays onto the road
A] Headlamp
B] Reflector
C] Lens
D] Adopter
225] To hold the bulb in the holder
A] Headlamp
B] Reflector
C] Lens
D] Adopter
226] To produce illumination
B] Reflector
C] Lens
D] Adopter
E] Bulb

227] To produce flat oval shaped beam

A] Headlamp

B] Reflector

C] Lens

D] Adopter

228] To hold the reflector in position

A] Headlamp

B] Reflector

C] Lens

D] Adopter

229] When the horn button is pressed the current flows to the horn from the....

A] dynamo

B] battery

C] starter

D] Horn button.

230] Horn sound waves are produced due to

A] Arcing in horn points

B] Vibration of diaphragm

C] Closing of points

D] Opening of points.

231] Horn relay consists terminals of

A] IBC

B] BPL

C] ABF

D] HBS

232] To make and break the horn circuit

A] Horn relay

B] Horn switch

C] Horn points

D] Solenoid

233] To operate the relay

A] Horn relay

B] Horn switch

C] Horn points

D] Solenoid

234] To increase the horn frequency

B] Horn switch

C] Horn points
D] Solenoid
E] Tone disc
235] To supply maximum current from the battery to the horn
A] Horn relay
B] Horn switch
C] Horn points
D] Solenoid
236] When the horn button is pressed the current flows to horn through
A] Horn switch
B] Solenoid coil
C] Battery
D] Chassis.
237] When the horn button is pressed the button touches the
A] Grounded plate
B] Live plate
C] Both
D] None of these.
238] Horn sound can be corrected by
A] Higher capacity battery
B] Adjusting screw
B] Use more no. horn
D] Using thick fuse.
239] Horn sound become poor due to
A] Sticky point
B] Discharged battery
C] Charged battery
D] Blown fuse.
240] Serves as passage for air
A] Air horn
B] Fuel bowl
C] Air cleaner
D] Air bleed
241] The wiper motor receives current from the
A] dynamo
B] Starter motor
C] cut-out
D] Battery.

242] The type of wiper unit used in present day vehicles is
A] <u>Electrical type</u>
B] Hydraulic
C] Vacuum
D] mechanical.
243] The wiper blades mating faces are made of
A] Leather
B] Fabric
C] <u>Rubber</u>
D] Fibre
244] Rotary movement to pull and push action
A] Wiper motor
B] <u>Cranking link</u>
C] Pinion
D] Wiper blade
245] Operates arm and blade
A] Wiper motor
B] Cranking link
C] <u>Pinion</u>
D] Wiper blade
246] Converts electrical energy into mechanical energy
A] <u>Wiper motor</u>
B] Cranking link
C] Pinion
D] Wiper blade
247] Causes oscillation of blade
B] Cranking link
C] Pinion
D] Wiper blade
E] <u>Cable</u>
248] Clears water layer from the glass
A] Wiper motor
B] Cranking link
C] Pinion
D] <u>Wiper blade</u>
280]The top and bottom halves of connecting rod are bolted on
A] crankshaft man journal
B] <u>crankpin journal</u>

C] camshaft
D] piston pin boss
281] A hole is drilled between crankshaft main journal and crank pin for
A] balancing of crankshaft
B] reducing crankshaft weight
C] lubricating connecting rod bearings
D] reducing crankshaft vibrations
282] Converts reciprocating motion into rotary motion
A] Crankshaft
B] Flywheels
C] Torque wrench
D] Thrust bearing
283] Rotary movement to pull and push action
A] Wiper motor
B] Cranking link
C] Pinion
D] Wiper blade
284] Accommodates wheel hub bearings.
A] Kingpin
B] Spring pad
C] Stub axle shaft portion
D] Track rod ball joints
285] Pushes with drawal plate
A] Clutch cover
B] Release bearing
C] Release fingers
D] Clutch plate
286] Takes thrust load
A] Crankshaft
B] Flywheels
C] Torque wrench
D] Thrust bearing
287]Distributor shaft is supported by
A] ball bearing
B] shell bearing
C] bush bearing
D] needle bearing
288] Stores energy

A] Crankshaft

B] Flywheels

C] Torque wrench

D] Thrust bearing

289] engages with the flywheel ring

A] Pinion

B] Over running clutch

C] Plunger disk

D] Clutch

290] Flywheel magneto consists of

A] Temporary magnet

B] Bar magnet

C] Permanent magnet

D] Needle magnet.

291] in flywheel magneto, the ignition coil is

A] stationary

B] Moving

C] Rotating

D] Oscillating.

292] To rotate the permanent magnet

A] Switch

B] Secondary coils

C] Flywheels

D] Condensers

293]The boiling temperature of the coolant in the cooling in the cooling system is increased by the use of

A]water jackets

B]vacuum valve only

C]pressure type radiator cap

D] radiator core tubes/pipes

INDUSTRIAL TRAINING INSTITUTE

Monthly Test-1, Marks- 20, Date:- _______________

(Every Question Carry Two Marks)

1-6] Used in gear box

A] Multi plate clutch

B] Dog clutch

C] Cone clutch

D] Diaphragm clutch

2-7] provides more frictional area
A] Multi plate clutch
B] Dog clutch
C] Cone clutch
D] Diaphragm clutch
3-8] smaller flywheel is used
A] Multi plate clutch
B] Dog clutch
C] Cone clutch
D] Diaphragm clutch
4-9] Spring acts as a release lever
A] Multi plate clutch
B] Dog clutch
C] Cone clutch
D] Diaphragm clutch
5-10] Type of drive mechanism
A] Pinion
B] Over running clutch
C] Plunger disk
D] Clutch
6-11] Prevents over speeding of pinion and armature
A] Pinion
B] Over running clutch
C] Plunger disk
D] Clutch
7-12] Engages with the flywheel ring
A] Pinion
B] Over running clutch
C] Plunger disk
D] Clutch
8-13] Connect two terminals of solenoid.
A] Pinion
B] Over running clutch
C] Plunger disk
D] Clutch
9-14] Double declutch IS not necessary
A] Sliding mesh
B] Synchromesh

C] Double declutching

D] Transfer case

10-15] Used in four-wheel drive vehicle

A] Sliding mesh

B] Synchromesh

C] Double declutching

D] Transfer case

INDUSTRIAL TRAINING INSTITUTE

Monthly Test-2, Marks- 20, Date:- ______________

(Every Question Carry Two Marks)

1-21] While reversing the vehicle the driver should control

A] Clutch

B] Forward gear

C] Accelerator

D] Hand brake.

2-22] The clutch plate assembly has a centre steel disc riveted with springs for

A] strength

B] flexibility

C] less noise

D] absorbing shocks

3-23] Dog clutches are used in

A] gear boxes

B] friction clutches

C] brakes

D] differentials

4-24] Synchromesh mechanisms is provided for

A] Increasing the speed of the vehicle

B] Reducing the speed of the vehicle

C] Smooth gear engagement'

D] None of the above.

5-25] Only spur gears are used

A] Sliding mesh

B] Synchromesh

C] Double declutching

D] Transfer case

6-26] Used for smooth gear shifting

A] Sliding mesh

B] Synchromesh
C] Double declutching
D] Transfer case
7-27] Hard gear shifting is due to
A] Worn out clutch disc
B] Damaged main shaft bearings
C] Synchronizer unit damaged
D] Excessive oil in the gearbox.
8-28] Gear slip is due to
A] Worn out synchroniser
B] Worn out clutch disc
C] Dry main shaft bearing
D] Weak pressure spring of clutch.
9-29] Noise in particular gear is due to
A] Insufficient clutch pedal free play
B] Damage gear teeth
C] Cracked gear box case
D] Damaged synchromesh unit.
10-30] Gearshift lever is used for
A] Releasing clutch
B] Changing gear
C] Increasing the speed of the engine
D] Controlling the direction of vehicle.

INDUSTRIAL TRAINING INSTITUTE

Monthly Test-3, Marks- 20, Date:- ______________

(Every Question Carry Two Marks)

1-36] which gears converts rotary motion into linear motion
A] worm gears
B] herring bone gear
C] rack & pinion
D] helical gear
2-37] What is a reason for gear slip
A] unlubricated gear linka-ges
B] less oil in gear box
C] broken teeth of gear
D] wrong adjustment of gear lever
3-38] In a differential gear ratio can be calculated from any one of the following statements

A] sun gear
B] planetary gear
C] crown wheel
D] pinion
4-39] low engine oil pressure may be due to
A] clogged oil filter
B] more oil filled in the oil sump
C] high viscosity of oil used
D] excessive backlash between pump gears
5-40] Increases road wheel torque
A] Engine
B] Clutches
C] Final drive
D] U joints
6-41] Used in four-wheel drive vehicle
A] Sliding mesh
B] Synchromesh
C] Double declutching
D] Transfer case
7-42] Four wheel drive should be used
A] Always
B] While climbing up hill
C] On sand (slushy ground)
D] While climbing down hill.
8-43] While driving in a wet or sandy roads always use
A] Four wheel drive only
B] Two wheel drive only
C] First gear only
D] More acceleration.
9-44] Fluid under pressures
A] To start heavy duty engine
B] Starter motor
C] Hydraulic cranking
D] Electric motor
10-45] Gasoline engine
A] To start heavy duty engine
B] Starter motor
C] Hydraulic cranking

D] Electric motor

INDUSTRIAL TRAINING INSTITUTE

Monthly Test-4, Marks- 20, Date:- _______________

(Every Question Carry Two Marks)

1-51] Allows fluid both way in and out of cylinder
A] Piston
B] Push Rod
C] Primary cup
D] Check valve
2-52] Seals the compensating port
A] Piston
B] Push Rod
C] Primary cup
D] Check valve
3-53] Actuates the piston
A] Piston
B] Push Rod
C] Primary cup
D] Check valve
4-54] Develops pressure on fluid
A] Piston
B] Push Rod
C] Primary cup
D] Check valve
5-55] Develops pressure on fuel to go out
A] Valves
B] Coil spring
C] Diaphragm
D] Rocker arm
6-56] Actuates the diaphragm
A] Valves
B] Coil spring
C] Diaphragm
D] Rocker arm
7-57] Allow fuel to flow in and out
A] Valves
B] Coil spring
C] Diaphragm

D] Rocker arm
8-58] Helps to return the diaphragm.
A] Valves
B] Coil spring
C] Diaphragm
D] Rocker arm
9-59] An overflow valve is used
A] to send back excess fuel from the fuel filler
B] to supply more fuel to the fuel filter
C] to supply clean fuel
D] to take the leaking fuel.
10-60] Excessive oil pressure in the lubrication system may be due to
A] less quantity of engine oil in sump
B] incorrect adjustment of relief valve
C] less suction effect on the suction pipe
D] none of the above

INDUSTRIAL TRAINING INSTITUTE

Monthly Test-5, Marks- 20, Date:- ______________

(Every Question Carry Two Marks)

1-66] Acts as a seat for spring mounting
A] Kingpin
B] Spring pad
C] Stub axle shaft portion
D] Track rod ball joints
2-67] Connects front axle with stub axle
A] Kingpin
B] Spring pad
C] Stub axle shaft portion
D] Track rod ball joints
3-68] Provides flexible movement for track rod
A] Kingpin
B] Spring pad
C] Stub axle shaft portion
D] Track rod ball joints
4-69] Accommodates wheel hub bearings.
A] Kingpin
B] Spring pad
C] Stub axle shaft portion

D] Track rod ball joints

5-70] Pivots on the bottom of frame and acts as a seat for spring

A] Upper control arm

B] Coil spring

C] Ball joints

D] Lower control arm

6-71] Acts as pivot for steering knuckle movement

A] Upper control arm

B] Coil spring

C] Ball joints

D] Lower control arm

7-72] Provides cushioning effect

A] Upper control arm

B] Coil spring

C] Ball joints

D] Lower control arm

8-73] Pivots on the top of frame and acts as a seat for spring

A] Upper control arm

B] Coil spring

C] Ball joints

D] Lower control arm

9-74] When front wheels are in straight ahead position and lines are drawn through king pins centre and steering arms end, at which point they will meet?

A] At centre of front axle

B] At centre of chassis

C] At centre of rear axle behind differential

D] At centre of rear axle just ahead of differential

10-75] Transmits its motion to meshing parts

A] Steering wheel

B] Worm

C] Steering column

D] Sector/roller/ball nut/peg

INDUSTRIAL TRAINING INSTITUTE

Monthly Test-6, Marks- 20, Date:- _______________

(Every Question Carry Two Marks)

1-81] The angle between tyre centre line and kingpin centre line

A] Negative camber angle

B] Positive caster angle
C] Kingpin inclination
D] Included angle vehicle
2-82] Tilt of kingpin towards centre of vehicle
A] Negative camber angle
B] Positive caster angle
C] Kingpin inclination
D] Included angle vehicle
3-83] In which type of steering gear box variable steering ration is achieved?
A] worm and roller steering gear
B] worm and nut steering gear
C] worm and sector steering gear
D] rack and pinion steering gear
4-84] A strut rod in a suspension is used in
A] conventional I beam axle type suspension
B] coil spring type suspension system
C] torsion bar suspension system
D] Macpherson system
5-85] Carries springs and steering linkages.
A] Front axle
B] Track rod
C] Stub axle
D] Stub axle arm
6-86] Acts as a seat for spring mounting
A] Kingpin
B] Spring pad
C] Stub axle shaft portion
D] Track rod ball joints
7-87] Pivots on the bottom of frame and acts as a seat for spring
A] Upper control arm
B] Coil spring
C] Ball joints
D] Lower control arm
8-88] Provides cushioning effect
A] Upper control arm
B] Coil spring
C] Ball joints

D] Lower control arm

9-89] in a Hotchkiss drive rear and driving torque is taken up by

A] rear axle housing

B] rear leaf spring

C] shock absorber

D] engine mountings

10-90] Helper spring is used in

A] Cars

B] jeep

C] light motor vehicle

D] heavy trucks

INDUSTRIAL TRAINING INSTITUTE

Monthly Test-7, Marks- 20, Date:- ______________

(Every Question Carry Two Marks)

1-96] Operates the cam

A] Brake pedal

B] Linkage

C] Cam

D] Pedal return spring

2-97] Operates the linkages

A] Brake pedal

B] Linkage

C] Cam

D] Pedal return spring

3-98] Supplies fluid to front and rear wheels

A] Brake pedal

B] Master cylinder piston

C] Wheel cylinder piston

D] Distribution block

4-99] Pushes the brake shoe towards drum

A] Brake pedal

B] Master cylinder piston

C] Wheel cylinder piston

D] Distribution block

5-100] Creates pressure on fluid

A] Brake pedal

B] Master cylinder piston

C] Wheel cylinder piston

D] Distribution block
6-101] Pushes master cylinder piston through linkages.
A] Brake pedal
B] Master cylinder piston
C] Wheel cylinder piston
D] Distribution block
7-102] Allows fluid both way in and out of cylinder
A] Piston
B] Push Rod
C] Primary cup
D] Check valve
8-103] Seals the compensating port
A] Piston
B] Push Rod
C] Primary cup
D] Check valve
9-104] Actuates the piston
A] Piston
B] Push Rod
C] Primary cup
D] Check valve
10-105] Develops pressure on fluid
A] Piston
B] Push Rod
C] Primary cup
D] Check valve

INDUSTRIAL TRAINING INSTITUTE

Monthly Test-8, Marks- 20, Date:- ______________

(Every Question Carry Two Marks)

1-111] For operating leading and trailing shoe brakes
A] Double piston wheel cylinder
B] Single piston wheel cylinder
C] Step-bore wheel cylinder
D] Baffle type wheel cylinders
2-112] Relieves excess pressure of air from the air tank.
A] Air compressor
B] Unloader valve
C] Safety valve

D] Brake chamber

3-113] Houses diaphragm and pushrod

A] Air compressor

B] Unloader valve

C] Safety valve

D] Brake chamber

4-114] Provides compressed air to system

A] Air compressor

B] Unloader valve

C] Safety valve

D] Brake chamber

5-115] Regulates maximum air pressure, reaching to air tank.

A] Air compressor

B] Unloader valve

C] Safety valve

D] Brake chamber

6-116] How brakes are applied in fail safe brake system during parking

A] by air pressure in brake actuator

B] By spring pressure in brake actuator

C] by vacuum in brake actuator

D] by mechanical hand brake

7-117] Supplies air to front and rear brake

A] Brake actuator

B] Dual brake valve

C] System protection valve

D] Flick valve

8-118] Operated for parking the vehicle.

A] Brake actuator

B] Dual brake valve

C] System protection valve

D] Flick valve

9-119] Exerts spring pressure and applies brake when air pressure in system is less

A] Brake actuator

B] Dual brake valve

C] System protection valve

D] Flick valve

10-120] Distributes air to various circuits

A] Brake actuator
B] Dual brake valve
C] System protection valve
D] Flick valve

INDUSTRIAL TRAINING INSTITUTE

Monthly Test-9, Marks- 20, Date:- ____________

(Every Question Carry Two Marks)

1-126] the tandem master has
A] two reservoirs and two outlets
B] one reservoir and two outlets
C] tow reservoir and one outlet
D] one reservoir and one outlet
2-127] Which defects of brake drum cannot be corrected by turning?
A] taper
B] over heating
C] ovality
D] scoring
3-128]The fluid pressure in a wheel cylinder can be increased by any one of the following methods
A] by changing dia of piston
B] by changing dia of rubber cup
C] by changing the spring
D] by interchanging of brake shoes
4-129] Air tank is made of
A]steel
B] copper
C] plastic
D] brass
5-130] Safety valve on air tank prevents
A] oil accumulation in air tank
B] excess air reaching to brake valve
C] bursting of air tank at high pressure
D] vehicle to move when brake has failed
6-131] How many air tanks are used in dual air brake system
A] one
B] two
C] three
D] four

7-132] Person acts as a steerman of the vehicle is called
A] conductor
B] Driver
C] Passenger
D] spectator.
8-133] Act for leaving the vehicle in dangerous position
A] 125 of MV ACT 1988
B] 126 of MV ACT 1988
C] 128 of MV ACT 1988
D] 122 of MV ACT 1988
9-134] Act for Riding on running board
B] 126 of MV ACT 1988
C] 128 of MV ACT 1988
D] 122 of MV ACT 1988
E] 123 of MV ACT 1988
10-135] Act for Obstruction of driver
A] 125 of MV ACT 1988
B] 126 of MV ACT 1988
C] 128 of MV ACT 1988
D] 122 of MV ACT 1988

INDUSTRIAL TRAINING INSTITUTE

Monthly Test-10, Marks- 20, Date:- ______________

(Every Question Carry Two Marks)

1-141] Delivers petrol to carburettor
A] Carburettor
B] Pump
C] Pipe lines
D] Petrol tank
2-142] Holds petrol
A] Air horn
B] Fuel bowl
C] Air cleaner
D] Air bleed
3-143] if petrol air mixture is compressed in a cylinder
A] its volume reduces
B] its pressure will rise
C] its temperature will increase
D] all the above will happen

4-144]During suction stroke the charge drawn in a petrol engine is
A] air only
B. air and petrol mixture
C] petrol only
D] fuels other than petrol
5-145] In a petrol engine air fuel mixture is drawn into the cylinder due to vacuum created during
A] power stroke
B] exhaust stroke
C] suction stroke
D] compression stroke
6-146] the high fuel consumption of a petrol engine may be due to
A] leakage of fuel from carburetor
B] defects in lubrication system
C] air leaks in intake manifold
D] incorrect idle speed (too low)
7-147] the float circuit is provided in a carburetor
A] to store fuel vapours
B] to supply mixture of air & fuel
C] to maintain proper level of fuel in float chamber
D] none of the above
8-148] increase or decrease the speed of the engine
B] Speedometer
C] Clutch pedal
D] Ignition switch
E] Accelerator
9-149] While allowing other vehicle to overtake
A] Accelerate
B] Reduce accelerator
C] Stop the vehicle
D] Move the vehicle to right.
10-150] Fuel catching fire
A] T.D.C.
B] Cycle
C] B.D.C.
D] Ignition

INDUSTRIAL TRAINING INSTITUTE

Monthly Test-11, Marks- 20, Date:- ______________

(Every Question Carry Two Marks)

1-156] Stores petrol
A] Carburettor
B] Pump
C] Pipe lines
D] Petrol tank

2-157] Delivers diesel to the engine
A] Carburettor
B] Pump
C] Pipe lines
D] Petrol tank

3-158] Delivers diesel to carburettor
A] Carburettor
B] Pump
C] Pipe lines
D] Petrol tank

4-159] Holds diesel
A] Air horn
B] Fuel bowl
C] Air cleaner
D] Air bleed

5-160] Serves as passage for air
A] Air horn
B] Fuel bowl
C] Air cleaner
D] Air bleed

6-161] Helps in breaking up fuel particles
A] Air horn
B] Fuel bowl
C] Air cleaner
D] Air bleed

7-162] Cleans the air entering the cylinder
A] Air horn
B] Fuel bowl
C] Air cleaner
D] Air bleed

8-163] Develops pressure on fuel to go out
A] Valves

B] Coil spring
C] Diaphragm
D] Rocker arm
9-164] Actuates the diaphragm
A] Valves
B] Coil spring
C] Diaphragm
D] Rocker arm
10-165] Allow fuel to flow in and out
A] Valves
B] Coil spring
C] Diaphragm
D] Rocker arm

INDUSTRIAL TRAINING INSTITUTE

Monthly Test-12, Marks- 20, Date:- ______________

(Every Question Carry Two Marks)

1-171] Limits the current to the points
A] Solenoid Switch
B] Actuating wire (when heated)
C] Ballast Resistors
D] Actuating wire (when cooled)
2-172] Closes the points
A] Solenoid Switch
B] Actuating wire (when heated)
C] Ballast Resistors
D] Actuating wire (when cooled)
3-173] Turns core to magnet
A] Solenoid Switch
B] Actuating wire (when heated)
C] Ballast Resistors
D] Actuating wire (when cooled)
4-174] Flywheel magneto consists of
A] Temporary magnet
B] Bar magnet
C] Permanent magnet
D] Needle magnet.
5-175] in flywheel magneto, the ignition coil is
A] stationary

B] Moving
C] Rotating
D] Oscillating.
6-176] To prevent arcing in the points
A] Switch
B] Secondary coils
C] Flywheels
D] Condensers
7-177] To complete primary circuit
A] Switch
B] Secondary coils
C] Flywheels
D] Condensers
8-178] To induce H.T. current
A] Switch
B] Secondary coils
C] Flywheels
D] Condensers
9-179] To rotate the permanent magnet
A] Switch
B] Secondary coils
C] Flywheels
D] Condensers
10-180] When the engine rotates the current is first produced in the
A] Secondary winding
B] Primary winding
C] Both the coil
D] Condenser

Printed by Libri Plureos GmbH in Hamburg,
Germany